Let's pretend we're
Sports Stars

Karen Bryant-Mole

First published in Great Britain by Heinemann Library, Halley Court, Jordan Hill, Oxford OX2 8EJ, a division of Reed Educational & Professional Publishing Ltd.

OXFORD FLORENCE PRAGUE MADRID ATHENS MELBOURNE AUCKLAND KUALA LUMPUR SINGAPORE TOKYO IBADAN NAIROBI KAMPALA JOHANNESBURG GABORONE PORTSMOUTH NH (USA) CHICAGO MEXICO CITY SAO PAULO

© BryantMole Books 1998

All rights reserved. No part of this publication may be reproduced, stored in a retrieval system, or transmitted in any form or by any means, electronic, mechanical, photocopying, recording, or otherwise without either the prior written permission of the Publishers or a licence permitting restricted copying in the United Kingdom issued by the Copyright Licensing Agency Ltd, 90 Tottenham Court Road, London W1P 9HE.

Designed by Jean Wheeler

Commissioned photography by Zul Mukhida

Produced by Colourpath Ltd., Soho.

Printed and bound in Italy by L.E.G.O.

02 01 00 99 98
10 9 8 7 6 5 4 3 2 1

ISBN 0 431 04657 3

This title is also available in a hardback library edition (ISBN 0 431 04656 5).

British Library Cataloguing in Publication Data
Bryant-Mole, Karen
Let's pretend we are sports stars
1.Athletes - Juvenile literature
2.Readers (Primary)
I.Title II.Sports stars
796

Words that appear in the text **in bold** can be found in the glossary.

Acknowledgements

The Publishers would like to thank the following for permission to reproduce photographs. James Davis Travel Photography; 17, Eye Ubiquitous; 7 and 15 Sean Aidan, Tony Stone Images; 5 Jon Gray, 9, 11 Steve Powell, 13 Tim Davis, 19 Mike Powell, 21 Lori Adamski Peek, 23 Amwell.

Every effort has been made to contact copyright holders of any material reproduced in this book. Any omissions will be rectified in subsequent printings if notice is given to the Publisher.

Contents

Tennis player 4
Hockey player 6
Runner 8
Racing driver 10
Basketball player 12
Horse rider 14
Skier 16
American Football player . 18
Golfer 20
Swimmer 22
Glossary 24
Index 24

Tennis player

Emily is pretending to be a tennis player.
She is about to hit the ball with her **racquet**.

Tennis is played on a court that is marked with white lines.
The white lines show the players whether the ball is in or out.

Hockey player

Naheed has made a pretend hockey stick. He is trying to hit the ball into a waste-paper basket.

These hockey players are wearing
shin pads inside their socks.
A knock from a real hockey stick can
be very painful.

Runner

Bartie is pretending that he has just finished running a marathon. A marathon is a very long race.

Runners who run short distances are sometimes called sprinters.
This sprint race has just begun.

Racing driver

Leila has made a racing car from a cardboard box. She is pretending to drive around a corner.

Racing drivers drive around a race track. They drive at top speed along the straight sections but slow down to go around corners.

Basketball player

Gemma is going to practise bouncing her basketball. Real basketball players have to practise, too.

Basketball is played by two teams. Each team tries to score points by putting the ball through a special hoop called a basket.

Horse rider

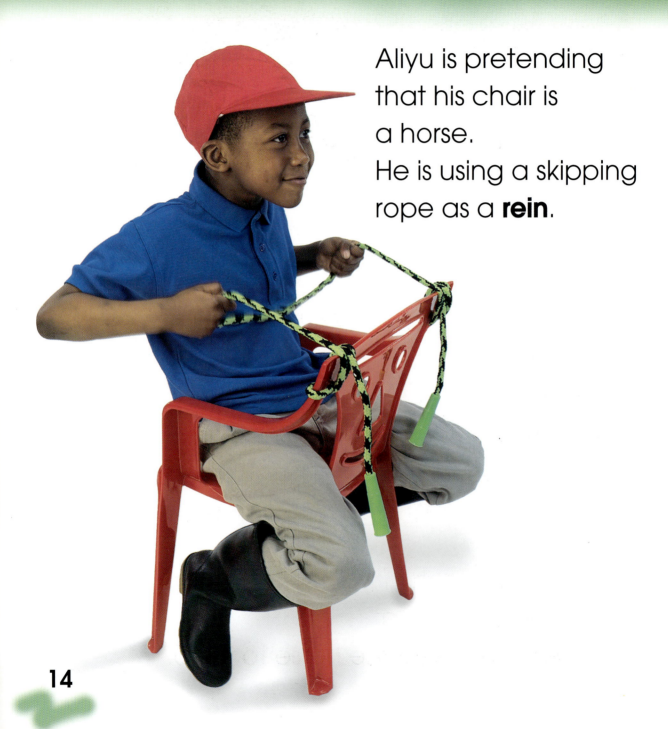

Aliyu is pretending that his chair is a horse.
He is using a skipping rope as a **rein**.

Horse riders use their legs and the rein to tell the horse what to do.
This rider has asked the horse to jump.

Skier

Leila is dressed as a skier. She bends her knees and crouches down. Real skiers do this when they want to ski fast.

This skier is in a slalom race.
As well as skiing fast, he has to ski around special posts, called gates.

American Football player

Edward is pretending to be an American Football player. He has padded out one of his big brother's T-shirts!

American Football players wear padded clothes to protect their bodies when they get **tackled**.

They wear helmets to protect their heads.

Golfer

Emily has a plastic golf set. She has some golf clubs, a golf ball and a special bag on wheels.

Golfers play on a golf course. There are some holes in the ground around the golf course. Golfers use different clubs to hit the ball from one hole to the next.

Swimmer

Naheed is pretending to be a swimmer. He is wearing flippers on his feet and goggles over his eyes.

This swimmer is wearing goggles, too.
They help her to see where she is going,
when her head is underwater.

Glossary

racquet a special type of bat

rein a strap that is fixed to a metal bar that goes inside a horse's mouth

shin pads pads that protect the bottom half of a sports player's legs

tackled when someone tries to get the ball

Index

American Football 18–19
balls 4, 5, 6, 12, 13, 20, 21
basketball 12–13
flippers 22
goggles 22, 23
golf 20–21
hockey 6–7
horse riding 14–15

padding 18, 19
racing cars 10–11
racquets 4
reins 14, 15
running 8–9
skiing 16–17
sprinters 9
swimming 22–23
teams 13
tennis 4–5